ABOUT MY DREAMS

SYED INAAM SHAH

Writers Desk

Writers Desk

Writers Desk

A GUIDING HAND TO BUDDING AND CREATIVE
WRITERS

A JOURNEY FROM WRITER TO AUTHOR.

Dedicated To

THIS BOOK IS DEDICATED TO THE VETERAN
QAWALI LEGEND USTAD NUSRAT FATEH ALI
KHAN

Foreword

"ABOUT MY DREAMS", IS A COMPILATION OF
COUPLETS, POEMS, MICROTALES, LETTERS, PROSE
AND QUOTES BASED ON LOVE, SEPERATION AND
SELF DISCOVERY.

YOU READ IT ANYWHERE, ANYTIME AND YOU WILL
CONNECT WITH IT IN ONE WAY OR THE OTHER.
IT WILL ALWAYS REMAIN YOUR ALLY AND
REMIND YOU OF WHO YOU TRUELY ARE

Acknowledgments

THE COMPLETION OF THIS UNDERTAKING COULD NOT HAVE BEEN POSSIBLE WITHOUT THE PARTICIPATION AND ASSISTANCE OF SO MANY PEOPLE WHO'S NAMES MAY NOT ALL BE ENUMERATED. EVERYONES CONTRIBUTION IS SINCERELY APPRECIATED AND GRATEFULLY ACKNOWLEDGED.

I AM PERPETUALLY GRATEFUL TO MY **PARENTS** AND MY **SIBLINGS** FOR THEIR SUPPORT AND WARMTH, FOR WITHOUT THEM THERE IS NO REAL MEANING TO MY LIFE.

I'M IN A LIFETIME DEBT TO MY ALL **FRIENDS** FOR THEIR CONSTANT BACKING AND LOVE.

SPECIAL THANKS TO THE "**WRITERS DESK**" FOR MAKING IT POSSIBLE FOR ME TO PUBLISH THIS BOOK AND ASSISTING ME DURING ALL ODDS

Poems

Oh, sorrow don't look daggers at my heart!

There are still red blotches in profusion

Now, life has no desires to live a new

Neither it has beats nor emotions

Alas! Turned into a wingless bird, who used to
fly in the spacious sky once.

But now dies over time

Whenever looks at the sky.

let me be ruined

Let the corpse of mine be decomposed

Let the pallbearers are allowed to carry me to
the cemetary

Oh, my shattered soul!

Don't fear from being disjoined

This was a peregrination,

Which we have expended in unison

And I bid adieu to thee for good

People's scare

World's annihilation

Oh, what a pity!

Now, Almighty! Please take pity on us!

Let us be stout that our unshakable faith will remain alive

Let us be immersed into your worship

Oh, formidable instant!

You are for the time being with us, forsooth.

Deovolente! You will be disappeared into thin air very soon.

I was frolicking by the lake

Where the daffodils were swaying in the breeze!

Oh what a lambent scene!

On the one hand, the comeliness of daffodils!

On the other hand, the comeliness if lake!

Under the shade of the tree, I sat next to them

And touched them gently

Never thought to pluck them

But, to look after them Jovially

At last, it remained a memory that still comes
like a wave of nostalgia.

Oh,sorrow! I am no longer living in that hope,

Which I had before

You smashed my heart

You left me restless during the days and sleepless during the nights

Alas! My beautiful life turned into a bad

condition

Neither I have peace of mind nor peace of heart.

Nature's love infinity

People enjoy heartily

Hurrah! What a bond!

Visits come and go

In mind, what are we feeling now?

Happiness! Happiness! Happiness!

No one can give us except nature's beauty where running water, snow, birds, meadow,and trees surround us.

in the murky night

I was in search of light to behold around that I

can feel I am not visionless.

let me imbibe a bitter brew that my heart cuts
will be mended from taking one after another
sip

I looked at the sky and the stars looked at me
we connected with each other!

After some time, rain fell

Stars went disappeared and I thought i was
dreaming.

I was in my garden and sniffing the fragrance of flowers oh!

What a moment when I was watching a swarm of Butterflies are sucking nectar.

oh, my happiness!

Where will I seek you out

You died a death by leaps and bounds

Neither you told me the name of your city

Nor said to me good bye!

Now, I came to you with my broken heart

Link to it with you!

Link to it with you!

Link to it with you!

The beauty of that land reminds me my

childhood

How beautifully decorated by me in my mind

Oh, my childhood!

Just come back once and take me to those
beautiful places where I often used to go.

Oh, man! dont debilitate your resolve

When you are falling victim to tight corners

Look at it like an ant,

Which sets foot in anything without fear.

the smiling corpse of mine,

Gone to darkness for good via pallbearers.

oh! My sorrow! You grew your thorns in abundance!

Now, my heart lets go of the rope of happiness.

Oh, man! Don't get a load of outer phiz

Which is pro tem!

And stay with you for the time being

By contrast, get a load of the inner beauty of
heart

Which is in perpetuum.

my heart is heavy with sorrow!

Not a single opening is there left for happiness

Now, I am gone into an out and out abyss

That I am peeping through my chest

Oh,hapless land of Kashmir!

There happened considerable inequity over your people!

Everyday you used to see corpses of innocent people on the shoulders of pallbearers

Alas! Thy land of paradise turned into hell

Where now these eyes are Witnessing the corpses of innocent people

These ears are hearing the sound of gunshots

These feet are walking towards the deserted places

These hands are begging like beggars

Now, with a hope

31

We are saying to you like this:

Switch back to paradise!

Switch back to paradise!

Switch back to paradise!

I sustain deep wounds from head to toe

When sorrow holds the nail in position and hammer it into my heart

In the martyrs' cemetery

The fragrance of Flowers scented the air

And I saw thousands of graves

As soon as I started reading their headstones.
My eyes burst into tears.

Oh, my shattered soul!

Why are you going repeatedly in search of healing before the merciless people!

For they came to you at one time for smashing you all!

Alas! There used to be a time, when people were tender_hearted not hard_hearted.

The din of the day

The stillness of the pitch dark

The chirping sound of the sparrows

The working of the people

The beauty of the nature

The fragrance and the thorns of the flowers

The tickling sound of the click

Quotes

38

He cries in silence

For not tolerating her absence

Happen he is dead deranged in love

But, doesn't know how

He goes through a period of how to be sans
her presence

And keep this very feeling in heart and this
very thought in mind

And by virtue of his perspective,

It is of the most essence.

He drinks venomous cup of feelings

And longs for wings

To reach to her at the very same time.

Bushy scabs at the hand of sorrow in my heart

by which, I seem to have lost my hope to live again.

The sufferings of heavenly vale

the bloodshed of Inculpable people

blood is found everywhere

alas! the cruels are still roaming freely

we have only heard the word "justice"

but still face injustice

we have only heard the world humanity

but still face "inhumanity"

we have only heard the word 'love'

but still face 'hatred'

we still don't ken where are we heading for?

this is still a rhetorical question.

Alas, I have been bound up

With my sorrow

that makes me feel low

my body so far

have received unhealed gashes

Now, I feel on my head,

multiple bashes,

My Eyes are shedding tears

to feed, my dry mouth

that I can couch

the storey of my hidden

scars in an isolated way

to the walls of my

desected house

Snowflakes are at full tilt

to spread over the ground

like a White blanket.

Where on we play, make Snowmen

do snowball fight

such a beauty live in this

blanket.

Be strong enough to make your mind
understand.

I see white ground

when i move around

oh, what a beautiful snowy

sight!

on which,i do fight

hurrah,i make footsteps

in fresh snow

that makes me happy now

If you are able to be patient,

so toughness too will

become easiness.

47

life is yours

be happy by having good thoughts

and be brave to face times of trouble.

nowadays, people's hearts

are having a want of

kindness

they love material

possessions more than

humans

alas! human values are

downgraded

people go to one another

when there is wedding or

condolence.

Disimiliar vexations in mind

as to how to be happy

Wherewith either our mind

will make us feel down

in the dumps or for bearing

how to live through it

snow is falling

My heart is crawling

while seeing through

the window the whiteness

of the world.

and I am not Shivering

with cold.

Hurrah! how snowflakes

lovingly fall to the ground!

By which, my heart longs

for going around

A cruel has opened out

his brutal claws over

the humanity.

Wherein, diabolical feelings,

Tenebrosity of heart, idiocy

of mind and dirtness of eyes

are met with himi

we have tuned out

our intellect

from therefore we

hold others liable,

art thou afraid of me?

aye, thy face bears a

resemblance to a blood curdling mutt

Nay, I dont Think forsooth

but thou Shouldnt keep thy.

fear in check and rub

thy eyes for identifying me

who am i!

54

Dissimilar vexations in my mind as to

how to be happy

wherewith either our mind will make

us feel down in the dumps Or

forbearing how to live through it.

My heart is a secluded garden

oft. times, visited by happiness,

and sorrow.

the former brings forth the

quality resonances and

the latter pops up a

Shedload of spines.

My heart wants to go

to a retired corner

Where darkness and

Absence of light will

De-stress me.

SYED INAAM SHAH

Live thy life not for kicks that

will bring transient hope

and get extinguished.

But conversely, live thy life

for trying to puzzle out

that will Really bring a

wave of bravery in thy heart

Wherein, Happiness positive

thoughts and patience and

the like.

Will be created inside thine

Own mind.

let me walk barefoot on hot ambers

that i can endure the pain.

Snow! snow! snow!

Not makes me feel low

I know now world is white

where we fight

hurrah! times seems beautiful

When snowflakes Fall to the ground

if you don't understand your own mind

so, it will become a life long suffering for you

world is beautiful if

you heartily spot it

world is nothing

if you sit idle

be like a river

that moves anywhere.

It is for sure

That my broken heart

still longs for cure

time was when this

received Unhealed gashes

by which, everything

trmed into ashes.

I am kind of confused to know

When people go to shrine to bow

Alas! They have, no belief in lord

by which life becomes odd

O, Mankind! hold the thread

of faith tight

that in your heart there will

be presence of light

My clothes became

Stained with blood

When I was picking up

dead bodless of innocent people.

eyes, became scary!

Hands Strarted to tremble

heart skipped to beat

of,Kashmir! My paradise!

Now, everything is gone .

Thy people lost their lives,

Thy land filled with blood

Sorrow has rooted in

In my heart

my mind lost its art

oh woe is me!

for I am going to fight

between my heart and mind

to find at once

If you love yourself

then you will never be

at the receiving end of

someone's taunt.

funerals are an everyday occurrence

in our paradise

no justice is given to the innocents

now, everyone seems in a dreadful

state

no hope, no prosperity,

no unity

as it seems to have turned our

paradise into hell.

Thy suffering wilt pain thee
if thou give up on thee.

In the luminous night,

I was Awake in My- room

Just for seeing Stars' Shine

No Sooner had 9 unclosed

the window than the

stars disappeared!

OH! What in excruciating

moment!

That left an abundance

of blotches in my heart

Which will never be

Mended.

oh, Grief! You wrecked the

beauty of my life.

Now, I am like a hollow

tree that has no

puissance to give birth t

o new leaves in the

Spring Season

Papers are witness to

my sore eyes!

When I fill them with

my grief

Oh,my dear mom! No one is more

Loyal than you

I always praise you for your

arduous task and courage

no one can take your place but

you.

Thou canst kill us

but not our courage

Thou canst choke us

but not our courage

Thou canst beat us up

but not our courage

Thou canst blind us

but not our courage

Thou canst lame us

but not our courage

Thou canst put us behind bars

but not our courage.

Birds are visiting my courtyard

and Chirping a lot for waking

me up everyday.

75

they jeered at my

simplicity

i picked upon

their wrong frame

of mind.

Melancholic days become

Bone parlous for my heart

and I kept on ululating

In Sorrow

cruel people blindfolded themselves

and took the lives of innocent people.

Alas! Floor Carpeted with blood

And got solidified

then voice came from their blood

that scared the cruel people.

We are united!

We are united!

We are united!

Oh, sorrow! Keep thy Waves

in check

in comparison to quondam ones

because my poor heart!

no longer Knows

how to go through thy

waves

let me Walk into the

abyss of darkness

Let me embrace the pesky

period of my life

Let me triumph over negativity

By having poositivity

In the murky might,

ı was ın search

of light to behold around

that I can feel, ı

am not visionless.

The din of the day

the stillness of the pitch-dark night

the chirping sound of the sparrows

the working of the people

the beauty of the nature

the fragrance and the thorns of the

flowers

the tickling sound of the clock.

About Author

Syed Inaam Shah hails from chattabal, Srinagar. He is 22 years old. Presently studying in final year in arts stream, He became very interested in writing and reading when he was studying in IST year. It created in him an art to pen down his emotions in the form of poetry and he always wanted to make his family proud especially his mother.

However, He also appreciate his mother, who always supported him in his tough times, hope you enjoy reading this book.